Arms
armo
Britain

Department of the Environment

Alan Borg

London: Her Majesty's Stationery Office

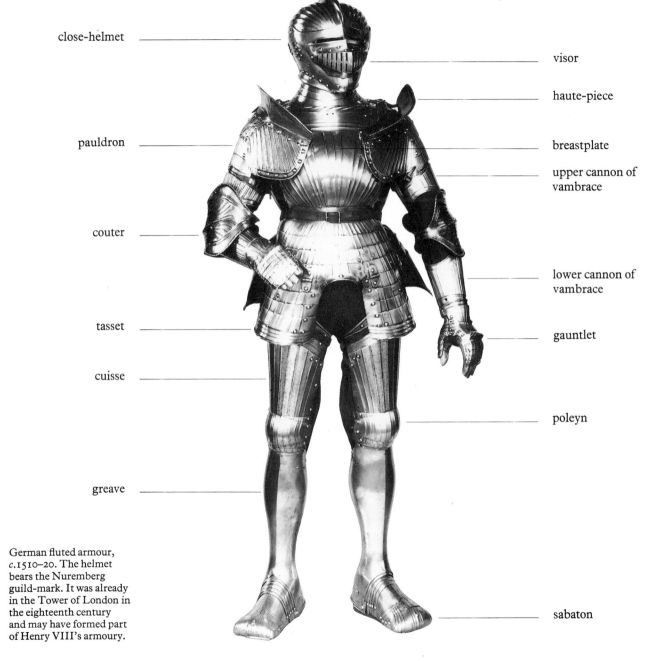

close-helmet

visor

haute-piece

pauldron

breastplate

upper cannon of vambrace

couter

lower cannon of vambrace

tasset

gauntlet

cuisse

poleyn

greave

sabaton

German fluted armour, c.1510–20. The helmet bears the Nuremberg guild-mark. It was already in the Tower of London in the eighteenth century and may have formed part of Henry VIII's armoury.

Foreword

The history of the parallel developments of arms and armour is extremely complex, since the competition between weapon smiths and armourers to surpass each other began several thousand years ago and still continues. This booklet is a brief outline of this story from about 1000 to about 1700.

The first edition of this book, then called *Arms and Armour in England*, (1960), was based on the contribution to *Medieval England*, (Oxford 1958) by the late Sir James Mann, KCVO, Master of the Armouries, 1939-62. The edition of 1969 was extensively revised by A. R. Dufty, Master of the Armouries, 1962-76. These two have served their purpose well but the time has come for an entirely new edition.

Unless otherwise stated in the captions, all the illustrations are of exhibits in the Armouries, H.M. Tower of London.

A V B Norman,
Master of the Armouries

English rapier, the hilt damascened with gold and encrusted with silver, *c.* 1635.

Arms and armour in Britain

It would be difficult to over-estimate the influence of arms and armour on the course of human development. Wars have punctuated history and often the violent death of an individual, of Harold at Hastings or Richard III at Bosworth, has changed the fate of nations. In the aristocratic and feudal societies of the Middle Ages the right to carry arms was a mark of social distinction, and the relative quality and expense of those arms was a subtle pointer to a man's position. The craft of the armourer was highly respected, and a finely made helmet or breastplate was generally regarded as the equal of a work of art. Indeed, during the Renaissance the decoration of arms and armour was recognised as a significant branch of the applied arts, and leading artists made designs for rich weapons or decorated fine armours. This is one reason why the study of arms and armour is both fascinating and instructive, for it is the study of objects that were made both to preserve and to enhance the life of their owner.

The important role of arms and armour in western civilisation can be seen and studied in countless illustrations of medieval manuscripts, in medieval and later effigies, and in oil paintings and engravings from the Renaissance onwards. Such illustrations are an invaluable source of information, but best of all is the study of the objects themselves preserved and displayed in museums and galleries, and nowhere better than in the old royal arsenal of the Tower of London.

It must be realised at the outset that the story of arms and armour in Britain is by no means the same as a history of arms and armour made in Britain. During the Middle Ages the finest armour and weapons were produced on the continent, mainly in southern Germany and northern Italy. Milan, Augsburg, and Nuremberg were among the most famous centres of armour production, while the sword blades of Passau and Solingen were equally well known. In London the Armourers' Company was founded by the fourteenth century, but it was not until the sixteenth that armours were produced in England which could compete with those of the continent in quality, design, and workmanship. At the same time it should be remembered that many of the weapons with which great battles were won, such as clothyard arrows and long hafted bills, were made in this country, by nameless village craftsmen.

Weapons, for hunting and for defence, were among the first tools used by man, and the most important single advance in their development came with the discovery of the malleability of metal, first bronze and then iron, in the fourth millenium B.C. Defensive armour evolved as a protection against man-made weapons, and throughout history there has been a constant attempt to develop the one over the other, a better sword necessitating a better armour and *vice versa*. But always the armourer has had to bear in mind practical questions, such as mobility and proper vision for the wearer. Most ancient cultures depended heavily on armed stength and consequently those which had the greatest influence on modern Europe, namely Greek and Roman, also laid the basis for the western

Detail of European mail, showing the construction of riveted rings.

development of arms and armour. For both the Greeks and the Romans armour normally consisted of a helmet, a cuirass covering the breast and back, and greaves protecting the shins. In addition to the solid plate cuirass the Romans also used the *lorica segmentata*, made up of strips of iron, fastened together with straps and hinges to give flexibility. A third type of body defence used by the Romans was mail, and this was to become the most common form in early medieval Europe.

Mail consists of interlinked iron rings. The rings are made from pieces of wire with the ends riveted together, although sometimes riveted rings alternate with solid rings (*page 4*). Mail can be made by simply butting the ends of the wire together, but this construction is obviously less strong and is normally only found in Oriental mail. Using this ring-technique a defence could be made in the form of a garment providing a flexible and effective protection; but it was heavy and hung as a dead weight from the points of suspension, normally the shoulders. Mail, however, had the advantage of being comparatively easy to produce, requiring only the repetitive actions of making and riveting the individual rings. The normal form of mail defence was a shirt, known as a byrnie or hauberk, which remained in use up to the late Middle Ages (*page 10*). During the Dark Ages warriors wore such shirts, with a helmet of iron for the head, and carried large shields for additional protection. Their main weapons were swords, spears, and axes. Little has survived from this early period, but some knowledge of the arms and armour of an Anglo-Saxon chieftain was provided by the discoveries in the great ship-mound at Sutton Hoo in Suffolk in 1937. This seventh century treasure included an iron helmet, decorated with panels of tinned bronze, clearly derived from a type used in the late Roman period, with a face mask, neck guard, and cheek pieces (*page 7*). There were also fragments of a hauberk of mail, a great round shield, and a sword.

The sword was the most important of weapons in the Middle Ages. A good sword was a priceless possession, and many famous blades were known by name and handed down from father to son. Equally, good smiths were highly regarded and at an early date it became common for smiths to sign their blades with their names or with their marks. A sound blade needed to be strong and sharp, but although it was known that a form of hardened iron (i.e. steel) could be produced by the carburization of iron the details of the process were little understood. Viking smiths overcame the problems by making blades from numerous strips of iron which were twisted and hammered out many times to ensure an even distribution of strength. The blades themselves are double edged, with a groove or fuller running down the centre; the fuller was intended to reduce the weight and to give the blade some flexibility, *not* to allow the blood to flow! The tips of the blades are rounded, indicating that the swords were used primarily as cutting rather than thrusting weapons. The guard consists of simple short quillons, and the pommel often has a characteristic tri-lobed or domed form (*page 7*). The grip was normally of wood bound with leather or wire, but since most surviving Viking swords have been excavated or found in rivers, the grip has nearly always perished, leaving the plain iron tang.

In addition to swords, Viking warriors carried axes and spears. The axes were fearsome weapons, with broad cutting edges; the blades often have a distinctive 'bearded' profile (*page 7*). Such was the association in the popular mind between these weapons and the Norse warriors, that for centuries afterwards the common name for a fighting axe was *Danish axe*.

The Norman knights who fought at Hastings were armed in much the same way as their Anglo-Saxon and Viking predecessors. However, there was one small but vital development, which affected the whole course of warfare. This was the introduction into Europe of the stirrup, first developed in the East. Stirrups began to be used in Europe during the eighth century, and it was soon realised that they gave a horseman a firm and

1. Helmet from the ship mound at Sutton Hoo, of iron inlaid with silver and with gilded and tinned ornaments. Seventh century (British Museum).
2. Viking axehead of 'bearded' form. Probably ninth century.
3. Viking stirrup found in the Thames, tenth century.
4. Viking sword, ninth century. The heavy black patination probably indicates that it is a river find.

1

2

3

4

7

certain seat, in which he could wield sword and lance with comparative ease and from which he could not easily be dislodged (*page 7*). The age of the cavalryman had arrived.

The equipment of the Normans is well known to us from the Bayeux Tapestry (*below*). This shows them wearing mail hauberks which reach to the knees, and Duke William and his half-brother Bishop Odo (for whom the tapestry was made) also wear mail stockings on their legs. The helmets are conical and fitted with a nasal bar at the front to give some protection to the face. The shields are large and kite-shaped, although some of the Anglo-Saxons are shown carrying round shields. Many of the soldiers wield axes, similar to those which the Vikings used, with swords and spears also much in evidence.

It has been mentioned that mail was heavy and rather uncomfortable to wear, and it could also be

5. Conical helmet, made up of separate pieces (Spangenhelm) Polish tenth century.
6. Detail of the Battle of Hastings from the Bayeux Tapestry. A Norman horseman reaches King Harold's standards. In the lower margin the dead are being stripped of their mail shirts. (After *The Bayeux Tapestry* Phaidon Press 1957.)
7. Sword of *c.*1200, with a wheel pommel and straight two-edged blade.
8. The rescue of Lot from the *Maciejowski Bible*, French, *c.*1250. On the right the Elamites, taken by surprise, hasten to put on their armour.

penetrated by lance or arrow. According to the epic *Song of Roland*, Archbishop Turpin's hauberk was pierced by four spears, but he still fought on. This may have been because it was normal to wear beneath the hauberk a sort of padded tunic, tightly stuffed with wool, known as a gambeson, which provided additional protection. Other materials such as hardened leather or whalebone were sometimes used for armour, as additions to rather than as replacements for mail. To judge from contemporary illustrations, mail remained the most common form of protection through the thirteenth and fourteenth centuries, and sepulchral effigies of mail-clad knights are still to be seen in many English churches. Sometimes sculptors and other artists adopted various simple conventions, such as wavy lines or repeated bands, to indicate that a figure was wearing mail, and it was once thought that these different conventions represented

different sorts of mail. However, modern studies show that all medieval mail was basically of the one sort, consisting of interlinked rings.

Norman swords were similar to those used by the Vikings, but during the twelfth and thirteenth centuries the blades were gradually made longer and so were the quillons. Most of the pommel shapes used by the Vikings continued in use, but a new type, the wheel or disc pommel, was introduced and became the most common form (*left*). Illustrations frequently show soldiers with falchions, which were swords with great curved blades, but very few of these have survived from the Middle Ages. Axes were still widely used; the blades were normally trumpet-shaped in profile and were set on hafts of four or five feet in length. The cavalry were armed with lances as well as swords while the infantry (which consisted of men lower down the social scale than

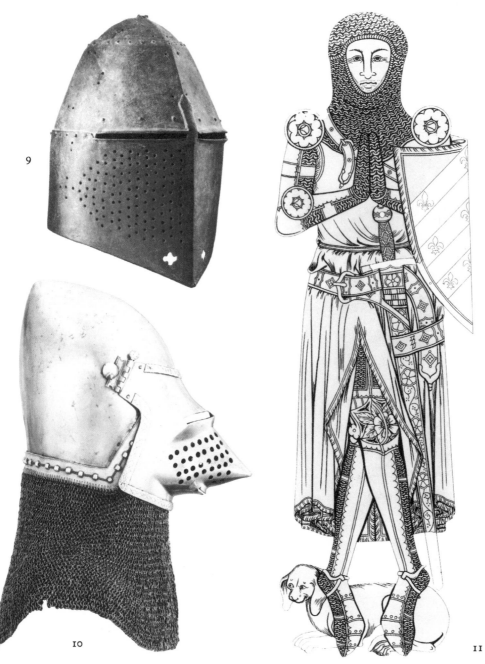

9

10

10

11

12

9. Great helm, probably English, c.1370.
10. Bascinet with visor and aventail, with engraved brass borders to the visor, North Italian, c.1380–1400.
11. Brass of Sir William Fitzralph, c. 1331-38, in Pebmarsh church, Essex, showing additions of plate armour to the limbs.
12. Mail shirt, traditionally that of Rudolph IV, Duke of Austria and Styria (1339–65).

the mounted knights) adopted a great variety of long hafted arms which could be used against both horse and foot. Some of these, such as bills, were adapted from agricultural instruments; others were developed from axes and spears and were given a variety of names, such as gisarme, glaive, vouge, and so on (*page 14*). It is also from the early twelfth century that we begin to hear stories of the power and deadly accuracy of the Welsh bowmen, whose descendants were to play such an important role in the great English victories of the Hundred Years War.

Although military equipment did not change radically during the twelfth and thirteenth centuries there were important changes in fashion. The mail hauberk remained standard but it tended to be worn shorter, ending above the knees, and was covered by a loose-fitting sleeveless gown which reached below the knees. The head was protected by a mail hood or coif worn over a padded arming cap. From the early thirteenth century an additional headpiece, the great helm, was worn in battle (*page 10*). This was of cylindrical form, with a flat top and horizontal slits for vision. At about the same time footsoldiers began to use a simple broad-brimmed iron helmet, known as a kettle hat. Shields became smaller and more triangular, with curved sides; and they began to be used for displaying heraldic devices. These devices were at first simply a means of recognition, for the knight, his head enclosed in a great helm, could not easily be identified. The *Nibelungenlied*, a twelfth century German epic poem, records how a Saxon knight fought with a man until he saw a crown painted on his shield and realised that his opponent was the hero Siegfried (whereupon he wisely surrendered). For the same reason distinctive crests were worn on the helms themselves, and illustrations show heraldic devices also on the ailettes, which were pieces of stiff leather strapped to the shoulders (*page 19*).

From the second half of the thirteenth century there are numerous references in literature and in documents to pieces of armour made not of mail but of plates of metal. It was realised that solid plate defences could provide much better protection than mail, the disadvantages of which have been discussed. Effigies and brasses of the period show how these defences were added to mail gradually, almost plate by plate, to protect especially vulnerable points, such as elbows and knees, and then to extend round the body until eventually complete plate armour was developed. It was a long process, but an early stage in the development can be seen on the brass of Sir William Fitzralph (*c.* 1331-38) in Pebmarsh Church, Essex (*page 10*). This shows simple plate defences strapped to the arms and legs and disc-shaped plates on the elbows and shoulders. The curving surfaces of metal plates could be used to advantage too, causing blows to glance off; realisation of this resulted also in the great helm being modified and given a domed rather than a flat top (*page 10*).

In the fourteenth century a new helmet, called the bascinet, began to replace the great helm for use in war, though the helm was retained for the tournament (see below). It was a close-fitting headpiece, covering the back of the neck and sides of the face, and rising to a rounded or pointed apex. The face opening was protected by a detachable visor, hinged to the helmet so that it could be raised or lowered as required. In the later fourteenth century these visors had a long, snouted appearance, giving rise to the English nickname Hounskull, or 'pig-faced bascinet' for a helmet of this type. Attached to the bascinet was a short cape of mail, the aventail, covering the lower part of the face and the shoulders (*page 10*).

Another important development was the appearance (or reappearance, since it was known to the Greeks and Romans) of the complete plate breastplate. For some time one form of body defence, as an alternative or addition to the mail hauberk, had been the coat of plates. This was a fabric garment lined on the inside with metal plates. Gradually these individual plates were joined together and the result was a rudimentary

13

breastplate, which still retained its fabric covering. Another change at this period was the general adoption of rowel spurs. Early spurs were of the simple prick form, and the rowel type, which had been known from at least the thirteenth century, only came into common use in the second quarter of the fourteenth century.

The arming of a knight in the late fourteenth century is well illustrated by the splendid tomb and funeral achievements of the Black Prince (d.1376) in Canterbury Cathedral (*left*). The tomb shows the prince wearing a bascinet, to which a mail aventail is attached. His head is resting on his great helm, which bears his lion crest. His arms and legs are enclosed in plate armour, the several small, carefully shaped plates or lames, which allowed movement at the joints, being accurately represented. His body is protected by a short hauberk over which he wears a tight-fitting jupon or coat of arms. In life, a jupon worn thus would conceal whether a knight was wearing a breastplate as well unless the curving outline, as here on the Black Prince's effigy, suggested that he was. Above the tomb hang the prince's 'achievements', including his actual helm and crest, jupon, shield, gauntlets, and the scabbard of his sword.

The development of plate armour was no doubt partly responsible for developments in weapons during this period. Sword blades were made to taper to a sharp point, so that they could be used for thrusting as well as cutting, and the grips were often lengthened so that the weapon could be used with two hands if necessary. For the latter reason these swords are usually referred to as hand-and-a-half or bastard swords (*right*). Daggers were also carried, by civilians as well as soldiers, and there were several distinct types in use (*page 13*). There were quillon daggers, not unlike miniature swords, and rondel daggers on which the guard and pommel were composed of flat discs. Especially popular in England was the ballock dagger, so called from the two lobes at the base of the grip, and this form remained in use until the

14

13. Gilt-bronze effigy of Edward, the Black Prince, d.1376, in Canterbury Cathedral, showing articulated plate armour for the limbs.

14. Hand-and-a-half sword, *c.*1420, with long grip and octagonal pommel. Found in the Thames.

15. A group of medieval daggers: (a) Ballock knife; (b) Basilard; (c) Rondel dagger; (d) Quillon dagger.

15a   15b   15c   15d

16

seventeenth century. The cavalryman still relied on his lance and sword, but for close in-fighting he might carry a mace as well (*above*). The infantry continued to use long hafted axes and bills, and bowmen now formed an important part of any English force. The English archers, who developed their skills on village greens, shot with a simple longbow of yew. When the bow stave broke or needed to be replaced it was simply thrown away, and so the most famous English fighting weapon

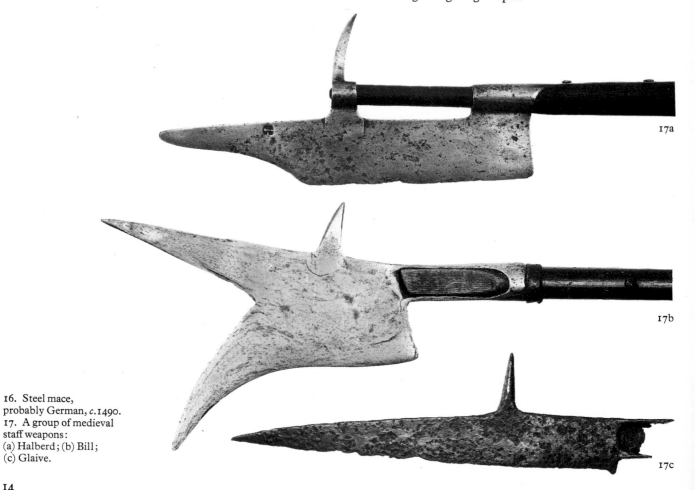

17a

17b

16. Steel mace, probably German, *c.*1490.
17. A group of medieval staff weapons:
(a) Halberd; (b) Bill;
(c) Glaive.

17c

18. Complete armour for horse and man; German c.1480. The horse armour was probably made to the order of Waldemar VI, Duke of Anhalt-Zerbst (1450–1508).

(Overleaf)
19. Siege of a town from Les Chroniques d'Angleterre, showing archers, crossbowmen, cannon and men-at-arms c.1480. (British Library. Royal Ms 14 E IV)

20. Water colour drawing of the armour of Sir John Smythe (1534–1607) in the *Jacob Album* preserved in the Victoria & Albert Museum. The surviving armour is illustrated on page 27.

is also today the rarest. There are some genuine longbow staves in the Tower which were recovered from the wreck of the *Mary Rose*, which went down off Spithead in 1545, and although they are of the Tudor period, they are of the same form as those which were used at Crecy and Agincourt.

The longbow was a simple instrument, only deadly in the hands of a skilled archer. On the contrary the crossbow, which was a complicated and expensive piece of equipment, required little skill in use; the bow, too strong to be drawn by hand alone, was mounted on a stock, and a variety of devices were used to span it (*below*). The simplest way was by muscle power, using an iron stirrup on the bow in which the foot was placed and drawing the cord by means of a hook hung from the belt by straightening the body, but levers, ratchets, and a complicated windlass system were also used. The result was a slow rate of discharge compared with that of the longbow, and crossbows seem to have been mainly used in England as siege defences and for hunting.

21

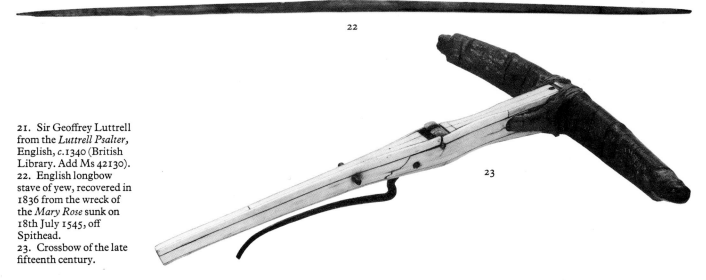

22

23

21. Sir Geoffrey Luttrell from the *Luttrell Psalter,* English, *c.*1340 (British Library. Add Ms 42130).
22. English longbow stave of yew, recovered in 1836 from the wreck of the *Mary Rose* sunk on 18th July 1545, off Spithead.
23. Crossbow of the late fifteenth century.

The fourteenth century was a period of transition in the history of armour, as plate was gradually added to mail. In the fifteenth century came the full development of plate armour, and some of the finest achievements of the armourer's craft date from this period. Certain families, such as the Missaglias of Milan or the Helmschmieds of Augsburg, produced armours of superb quality and style which rank among the finest achievements of late Gothic art. In England the supremacy of the continental armourers was not challenged, and the gentry who could afford to do so purchased their armour abroad. A fine illustration of this is provided by the effigy on the tomb of Richard Beauchamp, Earl of Warwick, dating from 1453, which shows the latest fashion of armour from Italy. A scale model of this armour can be seen in the Tower Armouries and can be used to show the equipment of a well armed knight of the mid fifteenth century. The torso is protected by a breast and back plate which is extended below the waist by a series of lames forming a skirt. Two plates, known as tassets, are hung from the skirt to cover the thighs. A pair of cuisses are strapped to the upper leg, and the knees are protected by poleyns. Greaves, made in two hinged pieces, completely enclose the shins and calves, and there are pointed sabatons for the feet, laminated to give flexibility. The shoulders are covered by pauldrons and the arm defences, or vambraces, consist of tubular upper and lower cannons joined by couters at the elbows. The head is completely enclosed in a new type of helmet known as an armet, which has hinged cheek-pieces locked at the chin and a moveable visor; it is surmounted by Warwick's swan crest. There is no shield, since the development of complete plate armour had made this defence obsolete.

The armour shown on the Beauchamp effigy is easily recognised as Italian from the characteristic rounded surfaces and smooth lines. German armour of the same period can be distinguished by its more angular style and fluted surfaces. Moreover, German armourers preferred a type of helmet, known as a sallet, which did not entirely enclose the head and had a long tail forming a neck guard. With a sallet, the chin could be protected by wearing a separate shaped plate defence called a bevor.

Thus armed, the knight was ready for battle. He was well protected but also had considerable freedom of movement. He was not unduly weighed down, for such an armour normally weighed around fifty pounds, evenly distributed over the body. He did not have to be lifted into his saddle with a crane (a persistent myth) nor did he remain on his back like a stranded beetle if he was knocked down. However, he probably did get very hot and uncomfortable if he had to wear and fight in his armour for long periods, and there are many stories of warriors who were killed when they raised their visors or removed their helmets for air. Consequently a knight only donned his complete armour when battle was imminent. In this he would be assisted by his squire, and a man could be fully armed within a matter of minutes if necessary.

The knight's horse too needed armour. In the fourteenth century this barding took the form of a mail trapper, but when plate armour was fully developed it consisted of a chanfron to protect the face, a crinet for the neck, laminated to permit movement, and additional plates for the breast (peytral), flanks (flanchards) and hindquarters (crupper).

It was also during the fifteenth century that jousts and tournaments became widely popular and that special types of armour were developed for sporting use. Nevertheless, mock combats had always been a standard way of acquiring skill in the use of arms, and the medieval tournament can be traced back to the Roman Troy Game (*Ludus Trojae*). During the twelfth century organised tournaments became more common, but they were regarded with suspicion by the authorities who saw them as both dangerous and seditious. The church repeatedly banned them, to no avail. In these early tournaments ordinary armour and weapons were used, with consequent loss of life, and so around

24. German gauntlets made at Landshut, *c.*1490.
25. Model by Peter Wroe, based on the effigy of Richard Beauchamp, Earl of Warwick (1381–1435) in St Mary's Church, Warwick. The effigy was cast in London by William Austen in 1453 and shows a Milanese armour of later fashion than would have been used by the Earl in his lifetime.
26. Rear view of the model of Richard Beauchamp.
27. (a) Sallet, North Italian (Milanese) *c.*1460; (b) Armet, North Italian (Milanese) *c.*1450; (c) Jousting Helm, known as the Brocas helm, S. German, *c.* 1490.

24

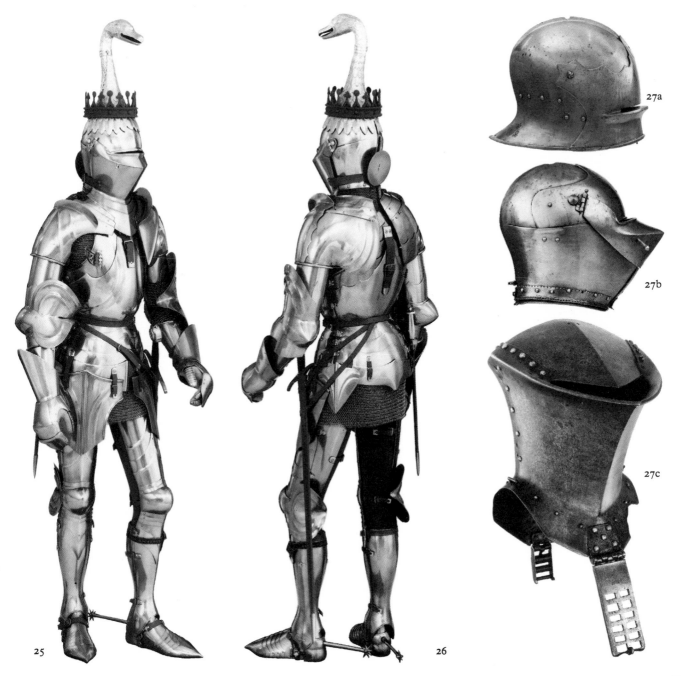

25

26

27a

27b

27c

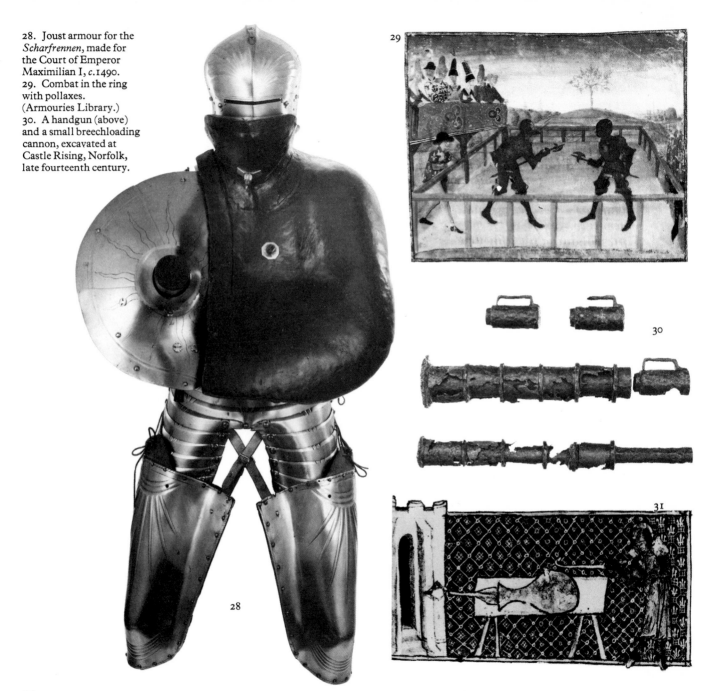

28. Joust armour for the *Scharfrennen*, made for the Court of Emperor Maximilian I, *c*.1490.
29. Combat in the ring with pollaxes. (Armouries Library.)
30. A handgun (above) and a small breechloading cannon, excavated at Castle Rising, Norfolk, late fourteenth century.

28

29

30

31

31. Early cannon from the manuscript treatise of Walter de Milemete *De Nobilitatibus, Sapientiis et Prudentiis Regum, c.*1326, in the Library at Christ Church, Oxford, showing a vase-shaped cannon, ejecting a javelin, touched off by a soldier armed like a knight, in a steel cap, mail shirt and surcoat and with heraldic ailettes.
32. English pollaxe late fifteenth century.

the year 1200 rebated or blunted lances came into use. It should be remembered that, strictly speaking, a tournament was a combat between groups of warriors, while a single combat was called a joust. The normal object of the contest was the splintering of lances or unhorsing. However, it was only in the fifteenth century that rules were really carefully defined and different sorts of contest established. Also, during the 1420s, a safety measure for the joust was introduced consisting of a barrier down the centre of the lists, which prevented the contestants from colliding. It was known as the tilt, and this form of jousting became known in England as tilting.

Different types of joust required different types of armour. The standard form of joust, known by its German name as the *Gestech*, involved the splintering of lances. For this the great helm was retained and given a characteristic 'frog-mouthed' shape. In one version of the German *Gestech* an extraordinary saddle was used, in which the knight stood rather than sat and was held in by wooden bars. Another type of joust, also primarily German, was the *Scharfrennen*, using pointed lances, and this clearly required a thick, heavy armour. A sallet was worn instead of a helm, a great semi-circular vamplate protected the lance arm, and a shield of wood and leather covered the left side of the body (*page 22*).

Mounted combats were not alone practised, and in England foot combats were very popular throughout the fifteenth and sixteenth centuries. In these the contestants fought in an enclosure (*champ clos*) and were fully armed. They carried a variety of weapons, but the main part of the contest was usually the exchange of a specified number of blows with swords or pollaxes (*page 22*). A variation was to fight over a barrier, when no leg harness was needed.

Pollaxes such as those used in foot combat could also be carried in battle (*left*), but in the late fifteenth century a new staff weapon was taken up by the English soldiery. This was the halberd, which had long been the weapon of the Swiss

infantry. By the time of its adoption by the English it had evolved its classic form, with an axe blade, a top spike and a rear fluke. Increasing use was also being made of pikes, which were simply long, small-bladed spears which could be formed into a hedge-like defence against cavalry. The other weapons of the common soldier, swords, daggers, bows, and so on, remained little changed, and probably few men were yet aware of the shattering new developments which gunpowder was already bringing about.

Cannon seem to have been first used in Europe in the fourteenth century, and the earliest illustration of one is in an English manuscript of 1326 (page 22). By the early fifteenth century they were a standard part of military equipment, especially in siege warfare. Hand guns were at first simply miniature cannon mounted on a wooden stock and fired by applying a lighted match at the touch hole (*page 22*). They were inaccurate, short ranged, and had a slow rate of fire; hardly, it seemed, a serious challenge to the bow. However, there were advantages, which, as the device improved, would make it supreme. It was simple to make and operate, did not require special skill or strength to fire, and the projectile could pierce steel armour. By the close of the fifteenth century hand guns were widely in use, although no mechanical firing system had yet been evolved. To cope with the recoil of the explosion of the larger hand guns the barrel was fitted with a hook which could be placed over a wall, absorbing the shock, and this type was known in Germany as a *Hakenbüsche*, which was anglicised as Arquebus.

In the field of arms and armour, no less than in the political and religious spheres, the reign of Henry VIII marks the close of the middle ages and the beginning of modern Britain. This was the last period in which complete armour was universally worn in battle by those who could afford it. The importance of guns in warfare was realised increasingly, with a consequent decline in the role of the armoured knight. This change was also deeply affected by the growing professionalism of war, which was rapidly becoming a contest between trained armies, fighting as a coherent force, rather than the pastime of the aristocracy supported by feudal levies. Nevertheless, armour was more than ever prized as a symbol of prestige, and tournaments of unparalleled splendour and display were held. The greatest European monarch of the day was the Emperor Maximilian, whose name is now used to describe the characteristic boldly fluted armours produced in the workshops of Germany and Italy during the early sixteenth century (*page 2*). King Henry in many was sought to emulate or outdo Maximilian in the extravagance of his court life, but there was one source of embarrassment: Henry had no royal workshops staffed by professional craftsmen to make him splendid armours, and when he received a present of an armour from the German emperor it must have galled him that he could not reply in kind. He therefore hired some Italian armourers and set them up to work at Southwark. This scheme failed, for unknown reasons, but a few years later, in 1515, Henry tried again, this time with German armourers and at Greenwich. The Italian experiment was obviously important, however, because one of the characteristics of Greenwich armour from the very beginning was the combination of German and Italian styles, producing a typically English result. Several features distinguish Greenwich armours; the pauldrons have a rounded, almost humped form, and are constructed of lames of equal size (unequal lames being normal on the continent). In addition, many constructional details, such as rivets and fastenings, can be used to characterise Greenwich workmanship. In the second half of the sixteenth century the helmets too can usually be distinguished by their prominent curving visors, resembling the prow of a ship; and there are many other small details that are distinctive of Greenwich work.

King Henry VII had decreed against livery and maintenance, prohibiting private armies, and for the same reasons Henry VIII ensured that the

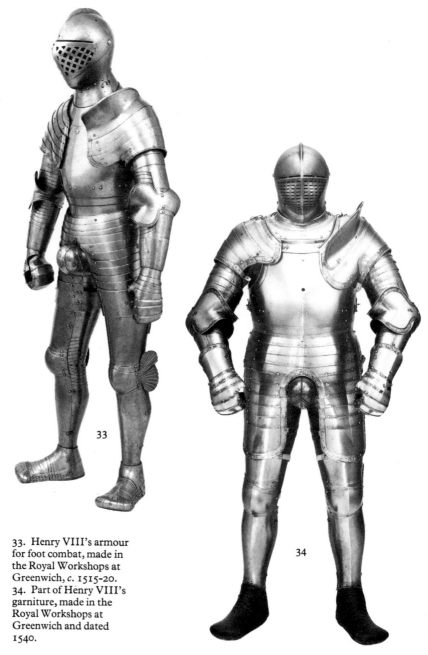

33. Henry VIII's armour for foot combat, made in the Royal Workshops at Greenwich, *c.* 1515-20.
34. Part of Henry VIII's garniture, made in the Royal Workshops at Greenwich and dated 1540.

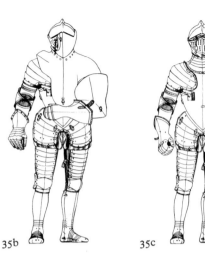

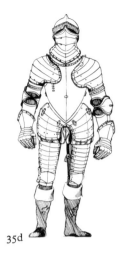

35a   35b   35c   35d   35e

35. Drawings showing some of the possible arrangements of a late sixteenth century Greenwich garniture. (a) Field; (b) the Joust; (c) Tournament; (d) Lancer; (e) Light horse or Infantry Captain.

Greenwich workshops only made armours by royal licence. In fact, the earliest surviving Greenwich armour was probably made for the King himself, for use in one of his favourite sports, foot combat (*page 24*). It may never have been finished, for it was originally black and rough from the hammer and was only made bright with repeated cleaning, but it is a masterpiece of the armourer's craft. This armour gives literally complete protection, enclosing the whole body in plates, with the individual lames moving on sliding rivets. It is a famous Tower comparison to move from this armour, made for an athletic young king, to another Greenwich harness, made for Henry in 1540, when he was an ageing and overweight tyrant (*page 24*). This gigantic armour also illustrates one of the specialities of the Greenwich smiths, a multi-purpose garniture which, by means of a series of interchangeable pieces, can be adapted for use in the field or in the tiltyard. This idea was also used by continental armourers, who produced small garnitures, using only a few exchange pieces, and large garnitures consisting of literally hundreds of pieces. Greenwich garnitures fall between these two extremes, and achieve the widest possible variations with the smallest number of pieces. The way in which the system

worked can be well illustrated with another Greenwich armour in the Tower, dating from the late sixteenth century, and shown here in some of its various possible arrangements (*above*).

In addition to establishing the Greenwich workshops, Henry VIII also surrounded himself with a great arsenal of weapons of all types. A great deal is known about this arsenal because it was included in the inventory of the king's possessions drawn up after his death in 1547, and it also forms the basis of the armouries collection at the Tower. It is clear that the King was well aware of the growing importance of guns. He had special cannon made in a foundry at Houndsditch and he also collected a range of experimental weapons, in which guns were combined with more traditional arms. A famous example is still known as Henry VIII's Walking Staff, which consists of a spiked club with three pistol barrels mounted in the head (*page 26*). Similarly there is a series of shields, each of which is fitted with a breech-loading gun (*page 26*). These guns worked on the matchlock system, in which a lever holding a lighted match was lowered into the touch-hole when the trigger was depressed. This simple system was used throughout the sixteenth and seventeenth centuries for military firearms, although a more sophisticated mechanism, the wheel-lock, was developed for fine guns. The latter, apparently the invention of Leonardo da Vinci, produced a spark through the action of a piece of iron pyrites against a revolving steel wheel. The pyrites was held on a pivoted arm and the wheel rotated by means of a spring, released by the trigger. It was a complicated and expensive type of lock, largely confined to rich sporting guns and pistols (*below*). Two surviving guns which were made for Henry VIII's own use were both originally fitted with wheel-locks.

Henry's gun-shields were probably made by an Italian, Giovanni Battista of Ravenna, and it seems that the king obtained much of his military equipment from Italy. The Armouries contain a large number of spears, partisans, and bills of Italian make, and these were probably carried by members of the various royal guards, for they are gilded and decorated with the royal arms and Tudor roses (*below right*). The King himself carried richly decorated swords and daggers, as Holbein's portraits of him show. Some of these were made by a Spanish artist called Diego de Caias, who also worked for the French King Henry II. One of the swords that Diego made for the King, richly decorated with gold damascening, is now preserved at Windsor Castle. It is a short sword for use in the hunt, known as a wood knife or hanger, and the quality of the work tells us much about both Diego's skill and Henry's taste.

The blade of the wood knife is decorated with an illustration of an historical event and one of the King's last military actions, the siege of Boulogne in 1544. It is said that during this siege wooden cannon were drawn up by the English to make the garrison believe that a great artillery force was facing them. One of these wooden cannon, called *Policy*, was kept in the Tower until it was destroyed by fire in 1841. The story is a perfect illustration of how far war had changed; the threat

38. Gun shield from Henry VIII's armoury, probably made by Giovanni Battista of Ravenna.

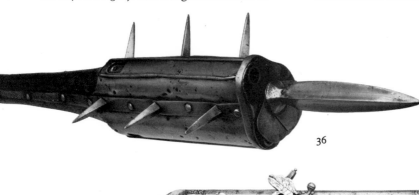

36. Henry VIII's Walking Staff. This is a type of spiked club known as a Holy Water Sprinkler, fitted with three guns in the head.

37. Richly decorated wheel-lock pistol, German, *c.*1580.

39. Staff weapons from Henry VIII's armoury, probably manufactured in Italy.

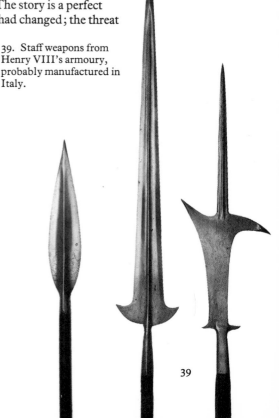

alone of superior fire power had become a formidable weapon. By this date complete armour was seldom seen on the battlefield and, especially on the continent, armourers devoted their skills to producing elaborately decorated armours for use in parades and displays, as well as for the tilt. The Tower Armouries contain a splendid example of such a parade armour, perhaps of French origin, the surface of which is embossed and damascened in gold (*right*). The art of embossing with the hammer required the greatest skill of the armourer, but at the same time it acknowledged the obsolescence of armour, for part of the protection had formerly been in the smooth, glancing surfaces of the steel.

The Greenwich armourers never went in for this very elaborate decorative work, and they continued to produce solid, workmanlike armours for use both in the field and in the tilt. However, on their richer field armours they did employ a characteristic recessed etched decoration. During the second half of the sixteenth century, under two queens, their work was done for the great courtiers of the land and many of their armours survive in the Tower. Several can also be seen in an important manuscript, preserved in the Victoria and Albert Museum, which contains water-coloured drawings of twenty nine Greenwich armours, together with the names of their owners (*right, page 18*). The book is believed to have been made sometime after 1588 by Jacob Halder, Master Workman at Greenwich from 1576-1607, and must be a sort of pattern or record book.

It quickly becomes apparent, both from Jacob's album and from the surviving suits, that armour was then closely following civilian fashion. Breastplates were drawn down to an ever more prominent point, echoing the peascod doublets, and the tassets bulged out from the waist to cover the voluminous breeches worn beneath.

Throughout the sixteenth century the commonest form of headpiece was known as a close helmet, which completely enclosed the face and had both a moveable visor and a bevor. The light cavalry

41. Armour of Sir John Smythe, made in the Royal Workshops at Greenwich *c*.1585, (see also page 18).

40

40. Parade armour, embossed and damascened with gold. Probably French *c*.1540.

41

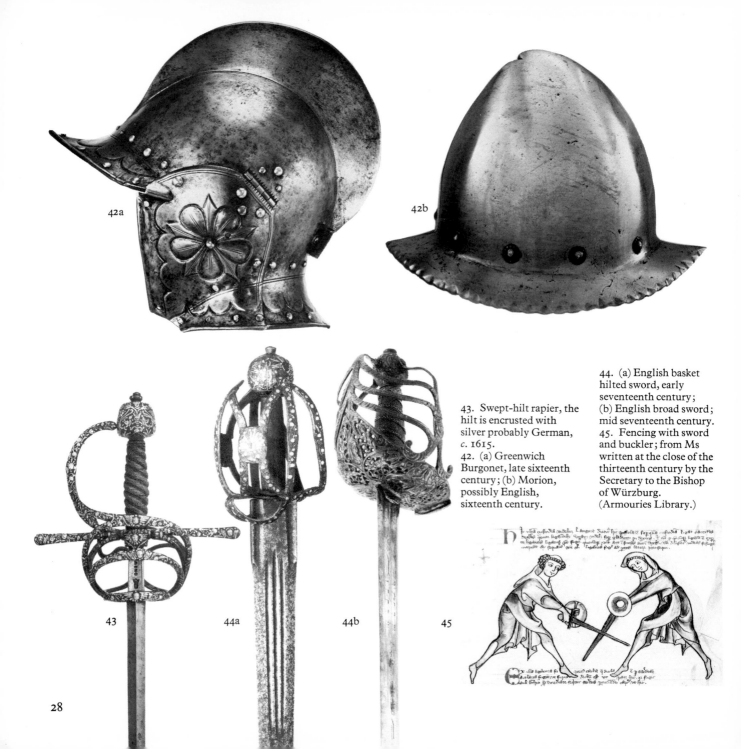

43. Swept-hilt rapier, the hilt is encrusted with silver probably German, c. 1615.

42. (a) Greenwich Burgonet, late sixteenth century; (b) Morion, possibly English, sixteenth century.

44. (a) English basket hilted sword, early seventeenth century; (b) English broad sword; mid seventeenth century.

45. Fencing with sword and buckler; from Ms written at the close of the thirteenth century by the Secretary to the Bishop of Würzburg. (Armouries Library.)

42a

42b

43

44a

44b

45

and infantry might wear burgonets, which were open-faced peaked helmets, while the medieval kettle hat had developed into the conical or combed morion, worn by the common soldiery (*page 28*).

The sixteenth century also saw the birth of the art of fencing. Sword play had indeed been practised for centuries, and in the Tower Armouries Library there is a thirteenth-century manuscript devoted to sword and buckler exercises (*page 28*). However, it was in Italy in the sixteenth century that a more refined system of fencing was evolved, in which parries were made with a dagger, carried in the left hand, and thrusts made with a long sword known as a rapier. Swords were then normally wielded in a gloved but not an armoured hand, and consequently sword guards became more complicated, with a system of bars giving protection. The classic rapier developed what is known as a 'swept hilt', and many such swords, which were worn with civilian dress, were beautifully and elaborately decorated (*page 28*). An English speciality seems to have been the encrustation of sword hilts with distinctive patterns in silver.

For use in warfare stout two-edged broad swords were still used, but these too were developing more complex guards, leading to the 'basket hilts' of the seventeenth and eighteenth centuries (*page 28*). Great two-handed swords were also carried, especially by the German mercenary troops known as Landsknechts, while in Scotland a characteristic type, the claymore, was used (*below*). The bow

had been largely replaced by the matchlock musket, yet in Elizabeth's reign there were still many who believed the bow to be the superior weapon. There was also a gradual abandonment of the long hafted weapons, such as bills and halberds, although decorated examples were still carried by ceremonial bodyguards, and the Yeomen of the Guard carry their partisans on state occasions to this day. The main long weapon still in use was the pike, and during the seventeenth century pikemen formed the core of the English infantry. A hedge of sixteen-foot pikes was designed to hold off an enemy charge, and so increasingly the technique of the cavalryman was to ride forward, discharge his pistols, turn and reload, without coming into direct contact with the enemy line. The pikemen were flanked by musketeers, whose job it was to bring down the charging cavalry.

The gun was already dominating the battlefield, and the evolution of a new type of lock in the late sixteenth century ensured that it would continue to do so. This was the snaphance and its closely related but more efficient development, the flintlock. It is a simple mechanism in which a piece of flint is held by a pivoted lever or cock; the cock is released by the trigger and swings down to strike the steel cover of the priming pan, forcing it back and at the same time causing a shower of sparks which ignite the powder. This lock was more efficient and easier to use than either the matchlock or wheel-lock systems, and it was to remain the normal form of gun mechanism until well into the nineteenth century. However, in the

46. Scottish claymore, mid sixteenth century.

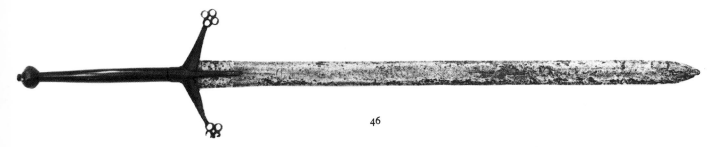

46

seventeenth century the matchlock musket was the type most commonly used by ordinary troops, while the flintlock was quickly adopted for pistols (*below*).

Full armour was now hardly ever worn in battle, but many troops continued to use half or threequarter armours, which gave some protection but did not restrict mobility. Two exceptions are the gilt and engraved armours made for Charles I and Charles II as Prince of Wales about 1640 (*right*). Light cavalry troops would probably wear open helmets, back and breast plates over a mid-thigh length buff coat which protected against sword cuts if not musket balls, and a long bridle gauntlet for the left hand. The heavy cavalry, which lasted but a short time in the seventeenth century, wore three-quarter armour, with long tassets reaching to the knees, and close helmets. Such cuirassiers would be armed with a pair of pistols, and stout swords, while the lancers naturally carried a lance in addition.

A favourite type of helmet worn in England during the seventeenth century by the light horse was known as a pot. The pot usually consisted of a skull piece, a broad laminated neck guard (hence the name 'lobster-tailed pot') and small cheek pieces. It was often fitted with a simple three-bar

47. Pair of flintlock officer's pistols, *c*.1650, by William Watson, Master of the Gunmakers Company 1644–9.
48. English matchlock musket, *c*.1630.
49. Harquebus armour of King James II made by Richard Hoden of London in 1686, shown here over a buff coat.
50. Armour of Prince Charles (b.1630), later Charles II, decorated with gilt bands and engraving.

49

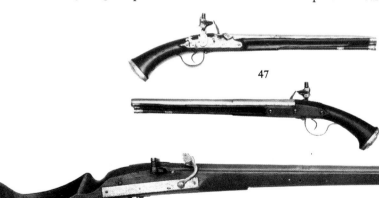

47

48

50

face guard. The pikemen wore a broad-brimmed pot-helmet and a short cuirass with solid plate tassets (see back cover).

These types of armour were worn by the forces of both sides during the Civil War, but there was a growing resistance to using any armour at all. As early as 1590 Sir John Smythe had complained that *our new-fantasied men of war do despise and scorn our ancient arming of ourselves both on horseback and on foot, saying that we armed ourselves in times past with too much armor, or 'pieces of iron' as they term it.* Three years later Sir Richard Hawkins lamented that he *had great preparation of armours as well of proofe as of light corseletts, yet not a man would use them but esteemed a pott of wine a better defence than any armour of proofe.* By armour of proof he meant armour which had been tested against gun shot, and many breastplates of the later sixteenth and seventeenth centuries bear a deeply indented proof mark of a musket or pistol ball. Inevitably, however, the better the proof the thicker and heavier the breastplate, and most soldiers preferred to trust their safety to mobility and luck.

By the time of the Civil War the Greenwich workshops had closed down, and by the end of the century most defensive armour had been completely abandoned and much of it had been returned to the stores in the Tower. The antiquary Francis Grose, who wrote the first historical study of armour in 1786, recorded that *cuirassiers are still to be found in most European armies; those of this kingdom must in future be supplied from old stores, the profession of an armourer being now totally extinct. The father of Mr Cooper of the armoury in the Tower was the last person regularly bred to that art.* In reality, the age of armour had ended well before Mr Cooper's father died, but it is fitting that the last English armourer should have been connected with the Tower, the place for so long associated with the history of arms and armour. Happily, too, Grose was wrong, for Mr Cooper's successors today preserve and restore the objects in the Tower collections and so keep alive the armourer's craft.

Where to see arms and armour in Britain

The national collection of arms and armour is housed in the Tower of London, where it has been since the sixteenth century. The galleries in the White Tower cover the development of military equipment and weapons from the early middle ages to the close of the seventeenth century and there are also special displays devoted to tournament armour and to sporting weapons. Many of the pieces illustrated in this booklet can be seen in the Tower. Also in London, the Wallace Collection houses a collection of medieval and renaissance arms and armour, including many examples of fine workmanship, and the Victoria and Albert Museum displays richly decorated arms. Later British military equipment can be seen at the National Army Museum. The collection of Her Majesty the Queen at Windsor Castle contains several important armours and many swords and firearms of the highest quality in pristine condition.

The arms and armour in the Glasgow Art Gallery and Museum, mostly bequeathed by the late R L Scott and the late C E Whitelaw, include some outstanding pieces, while in Edinburgh the National Museum of Antiquities of Scotland has an unrivalled collection of the weapons peculiar to Scotland. In addition to the collections in these and other museums, many castles and stately homes contain armouries.

The greatest armouries in Europe are in Vienna, Madrid, Dresden and Paris. In New York the Metropolitan Museum contains a comparatively newly-formed representative collection of very high quality.

51. Chanfron belonging with the armour of Robert Dudley, Earl of Leicester (1532 ?–88).

51